MW00684897

The Civil War Memoir
of William T. Levey

Edited by William F. Howard

Foreword by Harold Holzer

NORTHSHIRE
PRESS

4869 Main Street
P.O. Box 2200
Manchester Center, Vermont 05255
www.northshire.com/printondemand.php

Notes and Introduction © 2008 by William F. Howard
Foreword © 2008 by Harold Holzer

Cover by Heather Bellanca

Cover photograph: Private Amenzo Cady, who served in Company C
of the 134th New York Infantry. *(Photo: Courtesy of New York State
Military Museum and Veterans Research Center)*

ISBN: 978-1-60571-008-2
Library of Congress Control Number: 2008933891

Building Community, One Book at a Time
*This book was printed at the Northshire Bookstore, a family-owned,
independent bookstore in Manchester Center, Vermont, since 1976.
We are committed to excellence in bookselling.
The Northshire Bookstore's mission is to serve as a resource
for information, ideas, and entertainment
while honoring the needs of customers, staff, and community.*

Printed in the United States of America
using an Espresso Book Machine from On Demand Books

Contents

Foreword

By Harold Holzer

No conflict ever inspired as many writers, or intrigued as many readers, as the American Civil War.

Even while the battles raged, newspaper correspondents embedded with both Northern and Southern regiments filed eagerly read daily reports about the progress of the respective armies. By the time peace was restored, thanks to these and subsequent observers and commentators, the collective traumas of division, death, and destruction, followed by presidential assassination and mass mourning, had not only convulsed national life, but also informed collective memory. Writers and publishers pumped the literary fuel required to keep the campfires symbolically burning in Northern and Southern recollection. The immediate products of this outpouring—regimental histories, self-serving autobiographies, and on the visual front, popular prints and celebratory public art—not only found appreciative audiences, but helped sanctify the enormous loss in life and property. These products also helped propel and define sectional reconciliation, flawed as it was in its exclusion of African Americans from the equation of reunion. Yet the avalanche of material did little to douse reader interest. The more the books poured off the presses, the more the publishers enrolled new writers to produce new books. Readers have never lost their fascination for these stories.

For the last twenty years, in fact, the genre of Civil War recollection—never far from the front list of publishers' catalogues—has enjoyed an unexpected renaissance that approaches a golden age in the literature. Whether spurred by the popularity and influence of Ken Burns' monumental PBS series *The Civil War*, or by the unexpected but richly deserved acclaim afforded James M. McPherson's milestone book *Battle Cry of Freedom*, writers continue to mine lost or forgotten original material to the continued enlightenment of insatiable enthusiasts, students, and scholars. And the Civil War Sesquicentennial will not even begin until 2011.

Although New York State suffered no destruction during the Civil War—save for the convulsive draft riots that struck Manhattan in July 1863 (smaller versions of which afflicted other northern cities at the same time)—it has never lacked for writers and readers of the Civil War. Easily the most famous was Ulysses S. Grant, who retired to New York City after his presidency, then took to a small cabin not far from upstate Saratoga to finish his own *Personal Memoirs* while fighting a brave but hopeless battle against terminal cancer.

But Grant was not alone. Often forgotten in modern assessments of wartime sacrifice is the indisputable fact that New York sent more men and materiel to the defense of the Union than any other state. Most experts concur that the Empire State generated 17 percent of all the troops who fought in the federal ranks between 1861 and 1865, and lost more men—53,114—than any other. The state contributed more funds than any other to the prosecution of the war as well, and also generated new military technologies—rifled cannon at the gun foundry at Cold Spring, and ironclad warships at the shipyards in Brooklyn—that helped to crush the rebellion in the South. Back at home, meanwhile, New York increased its influence in molding Northern public opinion through the steady growth of its publishing industry: not only newspapers and prints, but among publishers who issued the first book-length histories of the war even while it continued to rage.

No less a symbol of the war than Lincoln himself recognized New York's crucial role in the Civil War by donating the handwritten draft of his Preliminary Emancipation Proclamation to one of the state's many fundraising charity fairs. Unlike the precious draft of the final proclamation—donated to Chicago and then burned in the city's great fire—New York repaid his generosity by lovingly preserving the hallowed relic in its state library.

The veterans of Lincoln's fight for union, majority rule, freedom, and equal opportunity contributed something precious as well: their recollections of the battles Lincoln had defined so eloquently, many of which almost magically retain their power to transport readers back to the transfiguring period that made America a nation.

One such memoirist was William Thomas Levey, whose long out-of-print recollections vivify a uniquely personal wartime experience—yet typify the bravery, sacrifice, and keen skills of observation so many soldier-writers brought to the task of preserving their experiences for future generations. Readers who continue to value their access to such priceless records owe a debt of thanks to William Howard for rediscovering this treasure and bringing it back into the spotlight where, deservedly, it shines anew.

Acknowledgments

Even slim volumes require the assistance of many people to help transform a book concept into a published book. First and foremost, I would like to express thanks to Chris Morrow and Lucy Gardner Carson at Northshire Press, based at the Northshire Bookstore in Manchester Center, Vermont, for agreeing to take on this project. The Northshire is an exciting place where people who love good books and the store's helpful bookselling staff will always find a happy marriage. Very special thanks to Master Bookseller Bill Lewis for good conversation and project support.

Recognition is also due to the legions of Civil War historians who have each added to my knowledge and understanding of Civil War history. The late Bruce Catton inspired me to pursue historical writing at an early age, and Clifford Dowdey, James McPherson, and Stephen H. Sears demonstrated that a good historian can produce solid history that is still interesting and accessible to the public. History, after all, belongs to all of us. Harold Holzer is a remarkable scholar and Lincoln expert who has been a friend and mentor for many years. Special credit is also due to George Conklin, who has carried the banner of the 134th New York Volunteer Infantry for many years and published a full-length regimental history as well as several articles on the unit's Civil War experience.

In addition, I would like to thank Michael Aikey, the Director of the New York State Military Museum and Veterans Research Center in Saratoga Springs, New

York. I am immensely proud of the museum and what it continues to do to preserve the history of New York's contribution to our nation's military heritage.

My family and friends have supported this project and shared some of the life of William T. Levey. I would like to thank my wife, Paulette E. Morgan, and my daughter, Katie Howard, as well as my parents, William G. and Laura Howard, for their support and assistance. Special thanks also to the staff at the New York State Library and State Archivist Christine Ward, as well as the dedicated board members and staff of the New York State Archives Partnership Trust.

William F. Howard
Delmar, New York
August 2008

Introduction

By William F. Howard

In 1903 a Civil War veteran named William Thomas
Levey (1840–1921) authored a series of newspaper
articles chronicling his experiences as a soldier in the
American Civil War.[i] The brief articles appeared in a
Schenectady, New York, newspaper and were well
received by a public anxious to know more about the
great events of 1861–1865. Because of their positive
reception, Levey was urged to compile all of the articles
and publish them together as a book. The resulting work,
entitled *The Blue and the Gray: A Sketch of Soldier Life in the
Army of the Civil War*, was privately printed by Roy
Burton Myers in 1904 but received only limited
distribution. Because it was bound in soft cover and
printed on inexpensive pulp paper, very few copies of
the book have survived.

Yet Levey's memoirs are of great value to Civil War
students. In a prose sometimes overly sentimental but
other times understated, Levey tells his personal story,
along with that of his regiment—the 134th New York
Volunteer Infantry—with honesty and candor. Patriotic
to the end and extremely proud of his military service,
Levey seemed haunted by the realization that a new
generation of Americans with no direct links to "the
war" might forget the sacrifices made by so many on the
smoke-filled battlefields of the 1860s. Levey composed
his story not so much as a personal memoir, but as a

tract pleading for a public remembrance of all who had fought and died beside him during four years of bloody conflict as well as a plea for unity and forgiveness toward those who had fought against him. Levey's inspiration—that in considering his words, a generation out of touch with its past might discover something worth remembering—is a concern that speaks to later generations as well.

When he was only 23 years old, William T. Levey enlisted as a private in Company H of Colonel Charles R. Coster's 134th New York Volunteer Infantry at Duanesburg, New York, on August 30, 1862. The regiment had been raised during the long summer of 1862 in Schoharie and Schenectady counties in upstate New York. After a series of devastating military reverses, President Lincoln had issued a call for 300,000 men to defend the Union and then had increased that number to 600,000. A generous enlistment bonus was being offered to those who would volunteer and fill the quotas assigned to the local communities. One advertisement published in the local newspaper offered an enlistment bonus of $152—at a time when privates were earning a monthly pay of $13. Like Levey, most of the men who served in the ranks of the 134th Infantry were farmers, born and raised in the community, but many of the men from Schenectady were skilled tradesmen and factory workers—enterprising immigrants from Germany, Ireland, Scotland, and France. The majority of the officers were prominent local men of political or wealthy influence who were able to secure commissions from the Governor. The men assembled at an impromptu encampment known as Camp Vedder, near the county fairgrounds at the small village of Schoharie, New York. By the end of September, enough men had been recruited to form a regiment and the awkward squad of would-be soldiers was mustered into service as the 134th New York Volunteer Infantry.

The regiment left camp on September 25, 1862, without much training or preparation, on orders from New York Governor Edwin D. Morgan. The unit was being rushed to Washington in response to the Lincoln Administration's desperate call for troops to defend the Capitol. Nearly a thousand men who formed the 134th Infantry left their homes for the march to Albany, participating in a disorganized and undisciplined procession to the State Capital. A contemporary newspaper account recalled:

> *It was on the 22nd of September in 1862 that I was down at Cold Springs near the Bozen Kill, gathering butternuts where you kids do today. Suddenly I heard the sound of music, and hurrying to the old plank road I saw the soldiers from Schoharie coming over the hill. With them were their ambulance and commissary train. Behind, riding in every conceivable conveyance, were their women-folks and children. Everyone in the neighborhood depleted the larder to feed the soldiers, who camped in the fields about Knowersville for the night. I can remember how my mother's heart went out to the crying, sobbing women and children who traveled so far to be with their loved ones. Some of the men were sick, quite a few got drunk, and eight deserted. In the morning they marched down the plank road to Albany.[ii]*

After enduring speeches, parades, and presentations, the regiment boarded a train for New York City and then left by boat for Washington on September 29th.

Like most of the soldiers who enlisted in the summer of 1862, Private Levey had volunteered to serve three years in the Union army. During his term of enlistment, he saw action in two of the Union Army of the Potomac's bloodiest fights, Chancellorsville and Gettysburg. At Gettysburg, the regiment was ordered to cover the retreat of the Union's 11th Corps and suffered the eighth-highest losses of the Union regiments engaged in the battle, losing 42 killed, 151 wounded, and 59 missing out of the roughly 400 men of the 134th Infantry who fought in the battle.[iii]

After fighting in some of the most important battles in the Eastern Theater, the 134th headed to the Deep South and, in 1864, participated in General William T. Sherman's famed "March to the Sea" during the Atlanta Campaign. Levey was severely wounded at Dug Gap, Georgia, on May 8, 1864, and was taken to a field hospital. He was forced to undergo the amputation of the lower portion of his left leg under the harshest of battlefield conditions. For several months Levey fought off the complications of gangrene and disease, never allowing his sufferings to weaken his spirit. Surviving his difficult ordeal, Levey was honorably discharged for disability from United States service on July 17, 1865.

Although he left the army a disabled veteran, Levey would never forget his role in the Civil War. He remained immensely proud of his regiment and ever loyal to the ideals that he had fought for. Modern-day historians will find no hints of scandal in his memoir, and there are no far-flung allegations of cowardice on the part of enlisted man or officer. Levey was writing his story for his hometown newspaper and maintained nothing but respect for his former comrades. It was only fitting: The 134th New York Infantry had suffered enough during the war. The regiment had been part of the Union Army's 11th Corps, a hard-luck organization composed primarily of German-speaking regiments that had taken its share of prejudiced slights and criticism during its service. At Chancellorsville, Virginia, in May 1863, the corps had been hit hard by a surprise Confederate flank attack led by Stonewall Jackson and had fled in panic from the battlefield. Early in the war, the corps had been commanded by Major General Franz Sigel, a political general appointed by Lincoln to appease German-American supporters. The corps' slogan, "I fights mit Sigel," was soon tossed back at them as a derisive counter, "I runs mit Sigel," in the weeks after the Chancellorsville debacle.

The troubled unit encountered still other problems on the battlefield that seemed to seal its reputation as problem corps. At Gettysburg, in July 1863, the unit had buckled under Confederate pressure and was part of the general rout of the Union Army on the battle's first day. Levey's regiment, deployed in a position north of the town, retreated as its position crumbled, retraced their original line of advance through the town, and ultimately established a new defensive position on Cemetery Hill, where the regiment's unit marker now proudly stands. Taken in this context, Levey's memoir is as much a soldier's personal recollection as a historical appeal in defense of the regiment of which he was so proud. In total, the regiment suffered some 500 casualties during its war service, including 4 officers and 59 enlisted men killed in action, another 26 who died of wounds received in action, and 3 officers and 91 enlisted men who perished from disease (19 as prisoners of war).

Not much is known of Levey's life after the Civil War. Census records indicate that he got married in 1866; he and his wife, Annie, produced four children, one of whom died early in his youth.[iv] Levey's occupation was listed as a "Laborer" in both the 1870 and the 1880 Census. A Special Census in 1890 that canvassed disabled soldiers and surviving widows of Civil War veterans found Levey living on Quaker Street in Duanesburg and noted that he had "lost a leg" and had been "shot through arm & leg." He and Annie last appear in the 1920 Census, with Levey's age listed as 79 and Annie's as 77. All of the children had moved out of the household by that time. A final public record for William T. Levey indicates that he died on February 9, 1921, at Delanson, New York.

Since I first discovered an original copy of Levey's memoir at an antique shop in the early 1980s, I have often found myself returning to its pages. Unlike many published memoirs of the war, Levey's unpolished and informal prose has always made me feel what it might have been like to sit at the knee of an old Civil War veteran and listen to the stories of camp and battle. Levey was a survivor of the war and of more trauma than he probably dared admit in his patriotic articles that formed this book. If his history is sometimes a little off or his phrasing a bit dated, it is in that conversational quality where Levey's slim volume achieves its great purpose. Of all of the memoirs, diaries, and personal accounts of Civil War service that I have studied over my long years of interest in this turbulent period of history,

Levey's is one of the best for giving the flavor of the impact that the selective memory of war had on an old soldier who fought the enemy on the battlefields of youth and then joined in fraternity and forgiveness toward his defeated enemy in the reflective final chapter of his long life. It is a remarkable story and a remarkable expression that has for too long been known only to historians or collectors of rare books and ephemera.

More than a century after its original publication, and eighty-seven years after the passing of its author, it is a great pleasure to once again make available the memoir of William T. Levey, for all of us who are interested in the great American epic that was the Civil War.

Notes

i. William Thomas Levey was born in Duanesburg, New York, on November 8, 1840, to Phillip and Monemia (McCollum) Levey. Levey was the third of seven children born to the couple, who lived on a small farm that the 1870 federal Census valued at $700. His father had been born in Schenectady in 1800 and his mother, in Scotland. William T. Levey died in Delanson, New York, on February 9, 1921.

ii. Account from the Esperance Historical Society Collection reprinted in George W. Conklin, "The Long March to Stevens Run: The 134th New York Volunteer Infantry at Gettysburg," *The Gettysburg Magazine.* Issue No. 21, p.46.

iii. John Busey and David G. Martin, *Regimental Strengths at Gettysburg*, Hightstown, New Jersey: Longstreet House, 1994, pp. 264–265.

iv. The 1900 Census lists three children living in the household of William and Annie A. Levey of Duanesburg, New York. They were William J. Levey, born in April 1867; Harry B. Levey, born in October 1880; and Charles J. Levey, born in December 1882. Another child, Albert E. Levey, age 5, is listed in the 1880 Census but does not appear elsewhere and probably died in his youth.

The Civil War Memoir
of William T. Levey

The Civil War Memoir
of William T. Levey

The 134th Regiment New York State Volunteers,[1] composed of young men from Schoharie and Schenectady counties, was mustered into the United States' service at Schoharie, New York, on the 22nd day of September, 1862.

Allen H. Jackson,[2] of Schenectady, was our Lieutenant-Colonel, and afterward became Colonel of the regiment. He was a brave and efficient officer and was much interested in the welfare of the men under his command.

He was taken prisoner at Gettysburg, but managed to slip away, and being swift on foot, he distanced his pursuers, clearing every obstacle in his way, and rejoined his regiment south of the town.

He has always been honored and respected by the members of his regiment, who were ever ready to grasp the hand of their gallant leader who cheered them onward to many victories.

Company H, of which I was a member, was fortunate in being under the command of Austin A. Yates,[3] a well-known and popular lawyer of Schenectady, New York, always a kind friend of the common soldier, ready and willing to share their hardships in camp or on the battlefield. He was loved and honored by his men, and he was much attached to them. The writer has known him for nearly half a century, and has always esteemed him highly. Indeed, he has a host of friends and admirers who have often listened with rapt attention to his cheerful voice and eloquent oratory.

Our encampment was on the Schoharie fairgrounds, where much of our time was spent in learning the many acts pertaining to military duty, and the deplorable art of so-called civilized warfare.

On our way to Albany we rested overnight at Knowersville, sleeping under the hotel sheds.

Arriving at Albany the next day we were given a good supper at the Delavan House,[4] then proceeded by rail to New York and then on to Philadelphia where we ate breakfast, then through Baltimore, to Washington.

Our first encampment was on Arlington Heights near one of the Lee mansions.

From there we went to Fairfax Court House, Virginia, where we had our first fight—a sham battle.

When in camp our time was occupied in drilling, target practice, guard duty, letter writing, cutting wood, carrying water, cooking, reading, cleaning muskets, and streets, washing clothing, etc. Our dishes and cooking utensils consisted of a tin plate, a knife and fork, a spoon and tin cup, and a light frying pan. The ground was generally our table.

When at the front our rations usually were salt pork, thick square crackers called hard tack, and coffee without milk or sugar.

While in camp we often had bread, fresh beef, desiccated vegetables, etc. For winter quarters we built small log cabins and stretched our tents over them for roofs, made a fireplace and chimney at one end with sticks and mud, and put brush on the ground to sleep on. Four to six comrades occupied a cabin. Jas. Waddell[5] of Duanesburgh, Charles Wood[6] of Guilderland, Wm. Mackey[7] of Schenectady, and J. Rockwell[8] of Esperance, were for a time my tentmates.

When on the march we often slept on the ground, rolled up in our blankets, and sometimes on stone heaps and rails to get out of the mud.

The fields of cotton when in full bloom were a beautiful sight.

Many of the buildings in the villages and on the farms were of logs.

Picket duty on the outposts was at times dangerous and often disagreeable. Rain or shine we had to stay two hours, keeping a close watch for the enemy until relieved by comrades from the reserve post a few rods distant. When on the picket line we always had a countersign, and if anyone approached he was ordered to halt and asked, "Who comes there?" If he answered, "A friend," we said, "Advance friend, and give the countersign." If correct he was allowed to pass; if not correct, or none could be given, we called the officer of the guard to arrest him. If he attempted to pass it was at his own peril, for it was our right to shoot him. If our outposts were attacked we returned the fire, and if necessary retreated toward camp until reinforced, then formed in battle line and fought like tigers to hold our position.

In passing over the Bull Run battleground we saw many graves of soldiers who were killed there in 1861, and so shallow were the graves and the covering that many bones were seen bleaching in the rains and sunshine of the Virginia clime. Buried where they had fallen, many of them far from home and kindred—brave men and boys in their teens—had fought, bled, and died for a cause which those of each side believed to be right and a duty they owed to the country they loved.

The Southern army had thrown up a line of breastworks at Bull Run and placed upon some of them stove pipes and logs, thinking to scare the Union Army with a great display of cannon.

One dark, rainy night we were aroused from our slumbers and ordered to pack knapsacks, strike tents, and go, we knew not where, but supposed it was to Fredericksburg to reinforce Burnside's army; and so it proved to be. Some of us were so sleepy we could not keep awake, and in passing by some camp fires they looked so inviting that we left the ranks and lying down by the fires, slept soundly until daylight, when we proceeded to our regiments at the front. On account of rain and mud, the fearful slaughter of the previous day was not renewed. Then the saucy Southern boys posted up for us to read, these words: *"Burnside Stuck in the Mud."*

The Battle of Chancellorsville, May 1863

The following spring we left camp about the first of May in heavy marching order, making thirty-five miles on a hot day. On our way we were fired upon by a masked battery one-half mile distant, most of the shells going over us and doing no harm. A company or cavalry was sent out and their guns were soon silenced.

That evening we formed our line of battle near a forest and rail fence. We worked late in the night carrying rails and digging trenches, making breastworks, etc.

When we had finished, General Von Steinwehr,[9] a funny Dutchman, rode along the line and said: "Now, poys, lie still und geep your eyes on dot fence by de voods, und ven you see de repels climb dot fence, rise oop and give'urn a wolley, und I pet you my life dey vill run like de devil." But they did not come, and the next day near sundown our brigade, under command of General Francis Barlow,[10] was ordered to leave everything on the field except our rifles and cartridges, and go on a reconnoitering expedition in the wilderness.

While we were in the dense forest a heavy roar of musketry was heard on the field. Some of our corps had stacked their guns near the timber and were preparing supper, when they were suddenly attacked by Stonewall Jackson's troops and driven partly across the field; but receiving support, they rallied and drove the "Gray Coats" back. Our knapsacks, tents, blankets, clothing, and rations were captured and burned. It became very dark before we found our way out of the forest and we moved very cautiously, as we were nearly surrounded by the foe.

On returning to the field we were told to lie down and rest, as the fighting had nearly ceased. A few shells were still flying over and bursting behind us.

About sunrise the next morning, which was the Sabbath, the enemy's artillery began firing as our brigade marched off the field to be held in reserve. Our troops were not all in line when the firing began, but they got there quickly. Officers were galloping their horses to and fro, infantry on double-quick, artillery and cavalry horses on the run—all getting in line for the battle that raged fiercely on that holy day. We expected at any moment to be ordered to face the deadly shot and shell. Then our thoughts flew homeward and to the church where we were taught to worship from our early childhood, and where our parents, sisters, brothers, and friends were perhaps seated on that eventful day. Oh! how we could appreciate such blessed privileges then, and we wondered how the Lord could tolerate anything so terrible in this enlightened Christian land. No tongue or pen can ever describe the sad heartaches and sufferings, the loneliness and desolation that is caused by the dreadful and sorrowful effects of war.

While this battle was in progress a heavy rainstorm came on and our troops re-crossed the Rappahannock River and went into camp at Brooke Station, Virginia,[11] each side claiming a victory and each army retreating at the same time.

The Battle of Gettysburg

It is not my purpose, nor will I attempt to say much in comparison to what might be said of a conflict of such vast proportions and long duration as that of Gettysburg. The story has been ably and fully told by practical and well-informed writers who were equal to the great task.

I have read accounts of the battle, and was told many particulars about it while there in 1902. I then made a memorandum of it and will merely state some of the most important acts and give as near as possible a correct statement of some of the parts taken by the first brigade, second division, eleventh corps; but in order to give a more precise and interesting account, I have made a few selections from history, which is often done, even by many practical writers, but I have rearranged and abbreviated to suit my own taste and ideas, adding, here and there, a few lines of a eulogistic and pathetic nature in connection with other portions original with myself.

The 134th New York was in charge of Lieutenant-Colonel A. H. Jackson, our Colonel, Charles R. Coster,[12] being in command of the 1st brigade.

Leaving Virginia in June 1863, General Robert E. Lee moved his forces on the west side of the Blue Ridge, while ours moved on the east side for the protection of Washington and Baltimore. While on this march, General Joseph Hooker resigned and General Meade was given command of the Union Army. We crossed the Potomac at Poolesville, Maryland, going via Middletown, Frederick City, and Emmitsburg. In the vicinity of these places is some of the finest country I ever saw.

On June 30th a company of Union cavalry entered Gettysburg. The citizens were much excited in regard to the coming battle, but as they gazed in wonder and admiration upon the long column of brave and gallant veterans with flashing sabres, glittering carbines, fluttering banners, and fiery steeds, moving proudly through their streets, they knew that it was the advance guard of a friendly and mighty host, the invincible Union Army, who would fight like demons to protect their lives and save their property from fire and plunder. This was the opening scene which later made the name of Gettysburg famous in history over all the world.

During the night of June 30th scouting parties informed our officers of the rapid concentration of a hostile force upon the town. The first shots were fired by the enemy upon General Buford's cavalry, our infantry and artillery having not yet arrived. Buford's men were hard pressed, as the fighting was fierce for an hour or more, when an officer saw in the distance the flag of General [John F.] Reynold's 1st Corps.

> *Now, said he, we'll hold the field.*
> *Hold the field, for Reynold's coming*
> *See his signal wave;*
> *Now we'll fight for freedom's right*
> *The Union we must save.*

Word was sent to [Major General Oliver Otis] Howard to hurry forward the 11th Corps. As the 1st Corps came on the field it was seen that the blue flag of the leading regiment bore the coat of arms of the Empire State—it was the gallant 76th New York. While leading the 1st and 11th Corps, General Reynolds received a fatal wound, fell from his horse, and almost instantly expired. At about eleven o'clock the fighting ceased for a few hours. The right now devolved upon Howard to take command of the entire field.

Steinwehr's division and [Captain Michael] Wiedrich's New York battery[13] were placed on Cemetery Hill, while [Major General Carl] Schurz's and Barlow's divisions were sent to the north of the town where another conflict was about to begin. These divisions included Coster's 1st brigade and were under command of General Doubleday.

The troops were now in line, forming a semi-circle. The enemy's artillery now opened their fire. The infantry advance to the attack. Soon the entire line, over two miles in length, is engaged. Over 45,000 men are in the deadly combat.

Through orchards and forest, over meadows and fields of ripening grain, nearly ready for the harvest, the gray line sweeps along with bold defiance and confident of victory.

The first attack was repulsed, resulting in severe loss to the Grays.

A regiment of true and valiant lads of the Keystone State went into action, shouting, "We have come to stay."

Alas! Too true with many of those noble youths who are yet there, lying beneath the blood-stained soil of their dear native state.

The 11th Corps struggled bravely against overpowering numbers, receiving the fire of both musketry and artillery, the latter enfilading their entire line, which was on the extreme right.

General Barlow was severely wounded and taken prisoner. One of Barlow's batteries of six pieces, under the command of a young officer only 19 years old[14] from New York State, held its position against sixteen of the enemy's cannon. The officer was fatally wounded and when dying, asked for a drink of water. As he received it, a comrade lying near him begged for a portion. It was given to him and he drank every drop. The young officer smiled, and then, far away from loved ones, deprived of their tender care and loving words, his brave spirit took its flight—away from the fields of strife and anguish, we trust, to peaceful and happy scenes beyond.

In this terrific contest our regiment lost over 200 men in killed[15] and wounded. The 154th New York,[16] of our brigade, also lost heavily, as both regiments were exposed in front and rear to a heavy fire from infantry and artillery. This was near the railroad station while covering the retreat of our troops through the town to Cemetery Hill.

A dead soldier of the 154th New York was found holding in his hand a picture of some children, and upon their faces his sightless eyes were still directed. He was a typical American soldier, in battle, brave and true; in death tender and loving.[17]

Some of the streets were strewn with dead and wounded men of both armies.

Many Union boys fought in sight of their own homes. Doors and windows were open and our tired and hungry veterans received refreshments from the hands of patriotic, generous, and sympathetic citizens.

Nearly 100 horses were killed in this first day's fight.

In the afternoon of July 2nd the contest was renewed, the enemy making the most desperate efforts to break a portion of our line extending from Little Round Top to the famous Peach Orchard, including the Devil's Den, Spangler's Spring, and the Wheatfield. The 44th New York Ellsworth regiment lost over 100 men here, in the defense of Little Round Top. General [Daniel] Sickles, who has done very much for our soldiers, was severely wounded and carried from the field.[18]

In the evening a fearful charge was made by the "Louisiana Tigers" upon the 11th Corps.[19] They were met with a shower of canister, but they rushed onward up to our lines, and then a fierce hand-to-hand fight ensued in which gunstocks, revolvers, swords, bayonets, and even stones were used. Our first brigade was conspicuous in routing the "Tigers" and saving Wiedrich's battery.

Our Commissary Sergeant, Sabe Smith,[20] of Braman's Corners, now came up with rations for our hungry and tired men, and during the night he assisted in caring for our wounded soldiers. He was afterward promoted to Acting Quartermaster of our regiment and then to Adjutant, and was mustered out at Albany, New York, as Captain of Company H, the company he enlisted in at Schoharie. He was a genial comrade and a competent official.

There was some fighting on a portion of the line until near midnight, and then the battle of the second day was closed.

Late in the evening, Meade called a council of war as to whether they should remain in that position, or retire to some other line. They finally decided to do as Slocum expressed it, "Stay and fight it out."[21]

All honor to that wise and skillful veteran commander of the 12th Army Corps—the corps that never lost a color or a gun. Always in the right place at the right time. Yes, indeed, we should all love and revere the name of Henry W. Slocum, a very gallant, noble, and illustrious benefactor, and son of the Empire State, whose remains are lying in the dark and silent tomb at Gettysburg;[22] but the memory of his brilliant and glorious achievements will continue to live in the hearts of a grateful and loving people, until his majestic monumental statue shall have crumbled into dust upon the consecrated soil of Gettysburg, and all things earthly shall have vanished forever.

Gettysburg on the Third Day

E re the dawn of the early morning of July 3rd had entirely changed places with the darkness of the night, the batteries of Slocum's 12th Corps began to boom in tones of thunder, sending their missies of death into the ranks of the enemy, some of whom were already in line, and awakening others who were yet sleeping. The battle raged with terrible effect until nearly noon, then quiet reigned for a few hours. Lee's artillery then began firing along his entire line. Our guns replied, and hundreds of cannon were then in action.

The constant and deafening roar was fearful and appalling—its equal was never witnessed on any field during the war. It was heard at the distance of forty miles.

And then the ghastly scenes of men and horses torn to pieces, while at times the pitiful cry of the wounded and dying horses could be heard.

The infantry on each side were lying on the ground. On our lines the men were intently watching. Soon the gray line was seen advancing from the timbers on the ridge. Their uniforms were not showy, nor their banners bright, for they had been carried many miles through dust and rain, had been cut and torn with shot and shell, and stained with the blood of many battles; but the line moved forward with such an air of precision and discipline that it aroused the admiration of our men who awaited their coming. They had to cross a valley about a mile wide. Our artillery inflicted much loss in their ranks, yet they moved steadily forward. A portion of our batteries reserved their fire until they came within close range, then nearly all began firing, and yet their progress was not retarded, until our infantry attacked them, and our cannon gave them terrific charges of grape and canister. And still some advanced up to the very mouth of our cannon; but they were met with such a murderous fire that several hundred threw down their guns and surrendered. Lee's loss in this action was very heavy.

A severe cavalry engagement took place, a few miles east of the town, between [Major General Judson] Kilpatrick's troops and the enemy, resulting in a victory for the "Blue Coats." 85,000 Union soldiers were at Gettysburg, and 27,000 of them were the sons of New York State.

The banners of our beautiful Empire State waved proudly amid the smoke of battle on every portion of that bloody field. During the fight the citizens sought safety in their cellars.

A young lady on Baltimore Street, who was making bread for our men, was killed by a stray bullet.[23]

Our total loss was about 23,000 in killed, wounded, and prisoners; Lee's loss was nearly the same.

Such undaunted courage and daring deeds of loyalty and devotion to country, has seldom been displayed on any field of battle, as was witnessed on those famous fields of Gettysburg.

On the eve of July 4th Lee's army began to wend its way back toward the "Green Fields of Virginia." His ambulances were filled with thousands of wounded. His wagon train was seven miles long, and a portion of it was captured by our cavalrymen. His men were disheartened by their failure; their bright visions were dispelled. The last ray of hope in their ultimate success had well-nigh fled, and their fondest dreams of the final victory which they had ardently and confidently expected would at last crown their heroic efforts, was now turning to dark despair.

Many of their dear comrades had been left behind, upon those deadly fields, where their blood had flowed in vain for a "lost cause," and the survivors were returning with sad hearts to the old camping grounds from whence they came.

Had Lee gained a victory at Gettysburg, he would have marched his triumphant legions over other parts of the north, even to New York State, but he was forced to return to Virginia, our troops following closely, inflicting losses to his army as opportunity offered.

The list of killed and mortally wounded in the 134th at Gettysburg was as follows: James H. Barkhuff, J. Barry, Christian Bentz, John Becker, Peter Bieber, Benjamin Bice, James Brownlee, Harvey Brown, John J. Buhler, Daniel Coton, James D. Cater, Jesse Chamberlain, George Chapman, John Connell, Robert Corl, Chas. Cosgreve, David Creighton, Philip Dana, John E. Dougal, George W. Douglas, Wilber N. Earl, James A. Ferguson, Jacob Geiser, John Grimm, Henry Glenn, David Haner, Leroy Hawkins, Ransom Hummel, William Huebner, John J. Hyart, James Jennings, Chas. Keller, Theo. Lemmer, Peter Link, J. A. Manchester, Wm. Martin, Lucius Mead, S. A. Miles, Nathan Nichols, Daniel Palmatier, Peter S. Palmer, Henry I. Palmer, Henry Peek, David S. Proper, George M. Reagles, Amasa Salisbury, John Shellkopf, Nelson Scripture, Wm. Slater, Joseph Schmidt, Fred Smith, Sylvanus Sweet, J. B. Thomas, Thurston Thomas, Cicero Tolles, John Tolles,

Jacob Trask, Robert Vaughn, Alonzo Van Arnum, C. Van Slyke, E. Van Dyke, A. K. Van Zandt, J. W. Vrooman, J. Watson, S. Wiedman, H. Wilber, P. C. Wilber. Captain W. E. Rockwell was captured and kept in Libby Prison over a year. He was a good and popular officer.

From Alexandria, Virginia, to Sherman's Epic March

In the autumn of 1863 we were stationed at Alexandria, Virginia, where we had easy times and good living.

We washed and bathed in the Potomac River, visited the city and saw the Marshall House, where Colonel [Elmer] Ellsworth was shot and killed by the hotel proprietor for hauling down a secession flag. The hotelman was immediately shot by one of our soldiers who stood near.[24]

Sometimes we got a pass to go outside of the camp lines, where we obtained milk, butter, biscuit, etc., of families living in the vicinity. We thus got acquainted with young ladies and had some jolly good visits with them, this was to us a very happy and agreeable change from the dull and irksome routine of military restraint and duty in camp and on the battlefield; and yet we had, at times, a little sport in camp.

This reminds me of an incident of a humorous nature that took place in one of the camps.

A Dutchman sat smoking his pipe, when a rifle ball from a sharp-shooter struck and broke it to atoms. He jumped up to get out of range, and said, "Now, see vot you done mit your tam nonsense—broke mine pipe."

From Alexandria we were transferred by rail to General Wm. T. Sherman's Army of the Cumberland. We passed through West Virginia, Ohio, Kentucky, Tennessee, and Alabama, and pitched our tents near Bridgeport, where we made corduroy roads, whereby our wagon trains might get to Chattanooga.

Now, some of the young readers may not know how corduroy roads are built; I will try to explain.

Small trees, from four to six inches in diameter, are cut down and placed lengthwise on the road, then other small trees or sticks are placed across them, close together and covered with brush, then finished by covering the whole with dirt.

In the forest trees of Alabama we picked sweet wild grapes as large as Concords.

After leaving Bridgeport on our way through Lookout Valley, we were attacked by both musketry and artillery and had to fight our way through to Chattanooga.

The women and children living in the valley were crying and screaming in terror for their lives.

The cannon balls and shells from Lookout Mountain made great havoc among the forest trees over our heads, but they could not train their pieces low enough to hit us, without bursting them, as we were near the foot of the mountain.

That night under cover of darkness, an attack was made on a portion of our corps, but, after a sharp fight, the Grays were defeated and driven back across a creek that separated the two armies.

One night while we were camping in this valley one of our sentinels on the picket line heard footsteps and cracking of brush. Thinking that the enemy were advancing, he fired his musket and retreated toward camp, giving the alarm. In an instant we were up and in line, ready to give them a very warm reception, but they did not appear, and we learned that it was a horse wandering about which caused the tumult.

The battle of Lookout Mountain and Mission Ridge was fought on the 24th and 25th of November, 1863— General W[illiam]. T. Sherman's army against General Bragg's and Beauregard's.

About this time the 11th and 12th Corps were consolidated and called the 20th Corps in command of General Joseph Hooker, a part of whose men led the attack on Lookout Mountain in the night and gained possession. This was called the "Battle Above the Clouds."

Early the next morning an advance of the entire line was ordered. The bullets from the enemy's picket line whistled sharply among us, as we drove them toward their main lines. We disturbed them before they had finished their breakfast, and in their hurry they left food and cooking utensils scattered over the ground in their camp. It seemed a pity to deprive them of their breakfast, but such are some of the discomforts and deprivations of war.

In the meantime a part of our troops were circling around the left wing of the opposing army, causing them to fall back, while the balance of us were fighting in front. Their lines were quickly broken, their rifle pits taken, and our impetuous and conquering heroes rushed onward and upward to the summit of the ridge, capturing artillery, and, turning it upon the fleeing enemy, firing into their ranks with their own cannon. Thus ended the battle of Chattanooga and Mission Ridge, giving us one of the most complete victories ever attained in the history of warfare.

After the noise and strife had ceased, we began to hear in the distance the loud hurrahs and joyous shouts of victory come ringing down the line, until it reached the ears of all our mighty host and reverberated over those picturesque hills and dales of "Sunny Tennessee."

This was, in my judgment, one of the best devised, best executed, and one of the most successful battles of the war.

We cannot give too much credit and honor to our bold and beloved Sherman, who led his army to many important victories. He possessed a master mind of great resource and strategy; and I have always been impressed with the belief that Uncle Billy, as we fondly called him, accomplished more with his intrepid and well-tried veterans toward ending the war, than did any other General in the entire Union Army. And that with a comparatively small loss of precious human lives.

After his victories in Tennessee, he made three divisions of his troops, in "Marching Through Georgia"—each division moving by a different route toward the sea, but within easy distance to reinforce each other if necessary in case of a battle. They conquered every obstacle before them, and fought successfully the battles of Rocky Face Ridge, Buzzard Roost, Tunnell Hill, Ringgold Station, Dallas, Lost Mountain, Kennesaw Mountain, Gulp's Farm, Peach Tree Creek, Stone Mountain, Atlanta, Chattahoochie River, Millidgeville,

Savannah, Jonesboro, North Carolina, and in conjunction with Grant's army, compelled the surrender of the Southern armies, near Raleigh, North Carolina.

In honor of my favorite General I quote a few lines of that popular old song, entitled "Sherman's March to the Sea":

> *Oh! proud was our Army that morning,*
> *That stood where the pine proudly towers,*
> *When Sherman said, 'Boys you are weary;*
> *This day, fair Savannah is ours,"*
> *Then sang we a song for our Chieftan,*
> *That echoed o'er river and lea;*
> *And the stars on our banner shone brighter,*
> *When Sherman marched down to the sea.*

Many thanks is due to my kind and courteous friend and comrade, F. Eisenmenger[25] of Schenectady, for the names of several places in Georgia where our regiment was engaged in battle, after I was wounded.

The citizens of Schenectady should be congratulated in having a felloe townsman so well qualified for the high official duties for which he has been chosen, and which he has so faithfully and honorably performed.

Mr. Eisenmenger is truly a gentleman whom it is a delight to honor and respect.

In the morning after our victory at Mission Ridge, the 20th Corps was ordered to Knoxville, Tennessee, for the relief of General Burnside's men, who were surrounded by General Longstreet's troops. But as we drew near, Longstreet's scouts informed him of our coming, and he withdrew his force from the place, thereby releasing Burnside's army.

Near Lewisville, we captured a train of cars, loaded with flour and meal, which I presume was intended for Longstreet's men, but we appropriated it to our own use, as it was just what we wanted for pancakes. We had to depend on getting our subsistence from the country while passing through it, as was often the case on long marches. After resting a day or two we returned to Chattanooga and built winter quarters.

A portion of us were barefoot, our shoes being worn out, and the railroad torn up, no supplies could reach us; the best we could do was to tie rags and handkerchiefs around our feet to protect them from the frosty earth and small pebbles.

There is seldom any snow in Tennessee, and the climate is very pleasant and salubrious.

At Chickamauga we captured some of the "Gray Coats," and among them was a young man who had formerly lived in Princetown, New York. When the war began, he was living in Tennessee. He joined the Southern army and fought against his Northern friends and the land of his birth. He was recognized by some of our regiment who had known him, and in conversing with him, we found that he was as bitter against the North, as if he had been born and bred a typical son of the South. Does it not seem strange? But so it was; even in some cases, father fighting against son, and brother against brother. What a sad and unnatural state of affairs to contemplate.

On the picket line in Lookout Valley the "Blue and the Gray" were in the habit of meeting on a partly burned bridge across the Wauhatchie Creek, that separated our lines, and trading sugar, coffee, and tobacco. The Grays generally had plenty of navy plug, but often no sugar nor coffee. We talked with them about the war, and they told us that we had the best gunners in our artillery, but they were going to whip us in the end.

The End

In May 1864 we moved southward and encountered the enemy on Rocky Face Ridge, Georgia. They were strongly fortified behind rock and trees. A sharp fight ensued, and we made a bayonet charge, but were driven back by heavy volleys of musketry, which thinned our ranks seriously. The loss in our regiment was 11 killed and 25 wounded. I recall the names of two who were killed near my side, Daniel Frederick[26] of Duanesburg and John Cornell[27] of Schenectady. Captain Edwin DeForest[28] of Schenectady was mortally wounded and died a few days later. The author of this story was severely wounded, and with others, taken to the Field Hospital at Ringgold, and then to Nashville, Tennessee, thence to Louisville, Kentucky. While there, my wound was attacked with gangrene, which had to be cut out, and then burned with bromine. I suffered intensely, became delirious, and my life hung as if by a single thread. I thank God that the thread did not break, and I am yet here to remind some of my readers of the sufferings and privations that thousands of patriotic youths endured for their benefit, that their homes and firesides might be protected from devastation, and themselves from violence in some cases, by the hands of a desperate and relentless foe.

It is to be regretted that there are yet a few inconsiderate people who have little or no regard for the soldier, who at his country's call, went forth in the vigor of early manhood, in defense of all the rights and possessions of every resident of the North, and of all the institutions of our beloved land; who fought, bled, and suffered to restore the Union with the comforts and security which are derived therefrom.

My friends and comrades, may the time be not far distant, when the soldier who wore either the Blue or the Gray (it matters not which, for we are all united now in the bonds of love and friendship) will be honored and respected by every resident in this country, from the Atlantic to the Pacific, and from the snow-clad mountains and icy coast of Maine to the tropical valleys and sunny clime of Mexico.

Let us rejoice, comrades, in the belief that a large majority of the people are our friends, and that we have their sincere and heartfelt gratitude for the support we gave to our country in its time of peril.

In the autumn of 1864 I had so far recovered from my wound, that I obtained leave of absence and visited my home.

In February 1865, I left Louisville with other comrades to join our regiments, going via Pittsburg and Harrisburg to New York, staying a few days at Castle Williams, on Governor's Island. We than went on board the steamer Illinois, bound for Beaufort, South Carolina. Soon after our arrival, the news came that Lee and Johnson had surrendered and the war was practically closed. Then our hearts were happy and light. We danced and shouted for joy. No more "Marching Through Georgia" with our invincible Sherman, but we would soon be marching homeward to enjoy the comforts and privileges for which we had fought on bloody fields of carnage, and to again engage in the pursuits of a peaceful and happy life.

On May 7th we left Beaufort, sailing northward, arriving at Washington [on] the 10th. We visited the Capitol with its elegant marble floors and magnificent oil paintings, the President's House, United States' Treasury, Patent Office, Museum, and other places of interest.

On July 17th, 1865, I received my discharge, having been in the service nearly three years.

Those of the readers who are not familiar with the remote causes which led to the Civil War should go back to a period soon after the Revolutionary War, and read the first and subsequent causes and events which finally culminated in a conflict so gigantic, so terrible, so destructive, and so sorrowful.

Although it caused widespread suffering and sorrow, thousands of heartbroken parents, wives, sons, daughters, sisters, brothers, and friends, over all our broad domain, in the loss of their loved ones, their wounded hearts find some consolation in the assurance that their lives were given in a just and noble cause, for the freedom and comfort of suffering humanity and the preservation of our glorious Union, which is now more permanent than ever, and we fondly hope will never more be threatened with disruption, but forever stand as a bulwark of protection to the advancement and prosperity of the most favored, intelligent, and patriotic nation on this terrestrial globe.

I had two brothers in the Union Army, James H. Levey,[29] who went from Brodhead, Wisconsin, as musician in the brass band, of which he was a part of the time the leader, and was with the Potomac army in Maryland and Virginia. Geo. A. Levey[30] of the 91st New York Volunteers was wounded at Gravely Run, Virginia, March 31st, 1865, and was in the hospital at Frederick City two months. He was then assigned to a position on the clerical force, in making out discharge papers and other documents in connection with the military service, until July 17th, 1865, when he also received his discharge papers and we returned home together.

To the youthful readers in particular, I yet have a few words to say: Endeavor to emulate the example of your patriotic ancestors, in cultivating your love and devotion to the dear old flag, the beautiful emblem of our nation's liberty and independence, which we trust may never again be assailed by foreign or domestic foe, or be lowered from the proud position it occupies in our hearts and over our loved homes, but it may continue to wave triumphantly until the end of time.

Now I must say a few farewell words to my brother soldiers, especially those who marched and fought side by side with me, and endured so much privation and suffering.

Dear comrades, we have long since fought our last fight in the armies of the Potomac and of the Cumberland, under the skillful leadership of such men as Sherman, Hooker, Meade, Slocum, and Howard.

But let us not forget that we have yet another conflict before us, of the utmost importance: We must battle against the wiles of sin, and the folly and snares which beset us on every side, and although we escaped the pangs of death upon the battle fields, there yet remains for us to face a death from which there is no escape.

We may never again cross the Potomac, the Rappahannock, or the Tennessee rivers, but we should lose no time in getting ready to cross that river, beyond which, it is said, there is a peaceful shining shore, where we may hope to meet with loved ones from whom we shall no more be separated.

Comrades, we are growing old; some of us, at least, will soon bid adieu to earthly scenes, and to those whom we so tenderly love, but if we have enlisted in the Army of our greatest Leader, and will fight bravely and faithfully under His banners we may finally win the most important and difficult battle of our lives.

Then when we march in triumph through the pearly gates and take possession of the Celestial City, we shall have gained our greatest victory.

We have all parted with those who were near and dear to us, and who are waiting for us beyond this vale of tears.

We hope to see them again. We have an intense and earnest desire to meet them in a happier home. Then why not be on the safe side and so live that we may avail ourselves of that greatest joy and eternal bliss.

Dear readers, comrades, and friends, some of you I may never see again on earth, but it is my earnest desire to meet you all in the realms of everlasting peace and joy.

Living in that fond hope, and trusting that it may be realized, I bid you all a kind farewell.

Notes

1. The 134th New York Volunteer Infantry was recruited in the counties of Schoharie, Schenectady, and Delaware and was organized at Schoharie to serve three years on September 22–23, 1862. According to the 1860 Census, the population of Schoharie and Schenectady Counties was 34,000 and 20,000, respectively. Most of the residents of the counties lived on small farms or in the close-knit villages that were spread throughout the rich agricultural valley. The city of Schenectady had a population of about 9,000. As of 1860, there were less than 750 African Americans living in the two counties.

2. Allan H. Jackson was a graduate of Union College and Harvard Law School. He had formerly served as a captain of Company G, 91st New York Volunteer Infantry. He was promoted to major on the field and staff of the 134th Infantry on February 23, 1863, and was mustered in as lieutenant-colonel of the regiment on March 10, 1863. He mustered out of service on December 11, 1865, but later joined the regular army and fought in the Indian Wars, rising to the rank of colonel.

3. Austin A. Yates was 26 years old when he enrolled at Schenectady to serve three years in the 134th. He was mustered in as a private in Company H on August 30, 1862, but soon rose to captain. He was discharged for disability, June 10, 1863, and saw subsequent service in the Veteran Reserve Corps.

4. The Delavan House stood at the foot of State Street in Albany and was owned by Edward Delavan, a noted abolitionist and temperance leader. The hotel served no alcoholic beverages and was frequented by many of the nation's elite. President Lincoln stayed here upon his visit to Albany in 1861.

5. Carried on the records as James McWaddell, a 21-year-old Duanesburg man who enlisted on August 25, 1862, and was mustered in as private, Company H. He was promoted corporal on September 22, 1862, but deserted the army at Falmouth on January 18, 1863.

6. Charles N. Wood, age 23 years, enlisted in the regiment on August 23, 1862, at Broome and was mustered in as private, Company D. He was discharged, January 12, 1863, at the U.S. Hospital.

7. William Mackey, age 23 years, enlisted at Duanesburg and was mustered in as private, Company H, on September 22, 1862. He was captured by the Confederates on April 3, 1865, near Goldsboro, North Carolina, but was quickly paroled. He was discharged June 23, 1865, at New York City.

8. Jay Rockwell, age 18 years, enlisted at Esperance on August 8, 1862. He was mustered in as private, Company H, and was later promoted to corporal. At Resaca, Georgia, on May 15, 1864, he was wounded in action. He was mustered out with his company on June 10, 1865.

9. Brigadier General Adolph Von Steinwehr (1822–1877) was a Prussian who had come to America to seek a military command during the Mexican War. He failed to gain a commission but returned to Europe with an American wife. Returning to America in the 1850s, he became a Connecticut farmer. At the outset of the Civil War he was commissioned colonel of the 29th New York Infantry and served in reserve at 1st Bull Run. He was engaged at 2nd Bull Run, Chancellorsville, and Gettysburg. Resigning from military service in 1865, he was later professor of military science at Yale and a U.S. government engineer.

10. Francis Channing Barlow (1834–1896) graduated first in his Harvard class. Although he had no previous military experience, he rose through the ranks to become one of the Union Army of the Potomac's most accomplished field commanders. He declined an officer's commission early in the war and, instead, enlisted as a private. He soon rose through the ranks and left military service in 1865 as a Major General. He was severely wounded at Antietam and was left for dead on the field at Gettysburg. He survived his wounds and went on to serve as Attorney General of New York after the war and headed the prosecution of the famed "Tweed Ring." He is also recognized as the founder of the American Bar Association.

11. Chancellorsville is regarded as a Confederate victory, although the battle cost the South the genius of General "Stonewall" Jackson, who died following complications

from an amputation after he was wounded during a nighttime patrol.

12. Charles R. Coster had already seen prior service with the regular army at age 24. He enrolled in the 134th at Washington, D.C., and was mustered in as colonel, October 8, 1862. He was discharged November 4, 1863.

13. Captain Michael Wiedrich led Battery I of the First New York Artillery.

14. The officer was Second Lieutenant Bayard Wilkeson (1843–1863), the son of *New York Tribune* correspondent Samuel Wilkeson. The officer commanded Battery G of the 4th United States Artillery at Gettysburg and was mortally wounded on the battle's first day. In a desperate condition on the battlefield, Wilkeson was forced to amputate his own leg with a pen knife. His father wrote a moving account of the battle and the loss of his son.

15. Actual losses were 42 killed, 151 wounded, 59 missing. In all the regiment lost a total of 252 out of 400 engaged.

16. The 154th New York under Colonel Patrick H. Jones was recruited in the counties of Chautaugua and Cattaraugus and was organized at Jamestown, New York, in the fall of 1862. The regiment was hotly engaged at Gettysburg on the first day of fighting and suffered severe losses.

17. Sergeant Amos Humiston was born in Oswego, New York, in 1830 and was Gettysburg's "unknown soldier." He served with the 154th New York Volunteer Infantry and was killed in action during the first day of the Gettysburg battle. His body was found near North Stratton Street in the town, still clutching a cased photograph of his three children, Franklin, Alice, and Frederick Humiston. In an effort to identify his remains, a national campaign was organized to publish the photograph in hopes that his identity could be discovered. The photograph was first published in the *Philadelphia Inquirer* on October 19, 1863, under the headline, "Whose Father Was He?" Eventually, Humiston's wife, Philinda, heard about the photograph and the postmaster in Portville, New York, notified the sponsors of the campaign. Humiston's wife was presented with the original photograph—still stained with her husband's blood—and reprints of the image were sold to raise funds for an orphanage established in Gettysburg for the children of the Civil War dead. Sergeant Humiston is buried in Grave 14, Row B, of the New York Section of the Soldiers National Cemetery in Gettysburg. The monument dedicated to him on North Stratton Street is the only monument on the Gettysburg battlefield devoted to an individual soldier.

18. Daniel E. Sickles (1825–1914) was a New York lawyer and legislator before the war who courted controversy throughout his long life. Sickles commanded the Army of the Potomac's Third Corps at Chancellorsville and at Gettysburg, earning the Congressional Medal of Honor for the latter battle. After

the war he was named chairman of the Gettysburg New York State Monuments Commission. When questioned long after the war as to why there was no monument to him on the battlefield, Sickles replied that "the whole damn battlefield is my monument." Considered a brave, if inept, military leader by many historians, Sickles was one of the last surviving general officers of the war and succeeded in crafting a Gettysburg history that served his own legacy to the detriment of many of his wartime colleagues. Sickles' leg was shattered by solid-shot cannonball and had to be amputated. The preserved relic is on display at the U.S. Army Medical College Museum in Washington, D.C.

19. This charge hit the Union position on Cemetery Hill and very nearly broke the tenuous defensive line General Howard had established. Today battlefield markers designate the high-water mark of this fierce action.

20. Listed in the records as Barney S. Smith, a 23-year-old who enlisted at Duanesburg and was mustered in as a private in Company H, on August 22, 1862.

21. This council was held in the one-room Leister House, which still stands near the visitors' center on Gettysburg battlefield.

22. Levey is in error here; Slocum was not interred at Gettysburg. The New York general died in Brooklyn on April 14, 1894, and was buried in Green Wood Cemetery.

23. Gettysburg legend recalls that Virginia "Jenny" Wade was baking bread when a stray rifle bullet came through the kitchen door and killed her. Miss Wade, who is buried in the civilian Evergreen Cemetery at Gettysburg, is believed to be the only Gettysburg citizen who died during the battle.

24. Elmer E. Ellsworth, a personal friend of President Lincoln, was killed by a shotgun blast to the heart fired by the hotel proprietor, James T. Jackson, on May 24, 1861. Ellsworth's bullet-riddled and bloodstained uniform is in the collection of the New York State Military Museum and Veterans Research Center in Saratoga Springs, New York. Sergeant Frank Brownell, of Ellsworth's regiment, avenged his colonel's death and killed Jackson. Ellsworth quickly became the North's first hero, a rallying point for all patriotic Northern youth. Jackson is still remembered in the South as a symbol of Southern defiance.

25. Ferdinand Eisenmenger, age 11 years, had been born in Prussia. He lied about his age and enlisted at Schenectady on January 16, 1864, and was mustered in as private, Company K. On January 25, 1864, he was appointed musician. Eisenmenger transferred to Company F, 102nd New York Infantry, on June 10, 1865. After the war he served as the Mayor of the City of Schenectady. He was the son of Ferdinand Eisenmenger, Senior, a 42-year-old man who also served in Company K who was wounded in action at Resaca, Georgia, on May 15, 1864, and later died of his wounds at Nashville Hospital.

26. Carried on the rolls as Daniel Fredericks, age 21, enlisted August 1, 1862, at Schenectady and mustered as private, Company H. Private Fredericks was killed in action at Rocky Face, Georgia, on May 8, 1864.

27. John Cornell, age 22 years, enlisted August 30, 1862, at Duanesburg and mustered in as private, Company H. Records list him as wounded at Gettysburg on July 1, 1863; he died of wounds received in action, July 10, 1863, in a hospital in Philadelphia, Pennsylvania.

28. Records carry him as Captain Edwin Forrest, age 28, enrolled at Albany and mustered in as first lieutenant, Company I, December 12, 1862, promoted to captain, Company B, February 13, 1864. Forrest was wounded in action on May 8, 1864, at Rocky Faced Ridge, Georgia, and later died of his wounds, May 18, 1864. The GAR post in Schenectady was named in his honor.

29. No record could be found of James H. Levey in the New York Adjutant General's reports.

30. George A. Levey is listed on the regimental rolls as "Leary." Records describe him as 18 years old. Enlisted at Schenectady and mustered in as private, Company H, 91st New York Infantry, on May 23, 1864. He was discharged at Washington, D.C., on July 12, 1865.

Bibliography

Boatner III, Mark. *The Civil War Dictionary.* New York: David McKay Company, 1988.

Busey, John W. and David G. Martin. *Regimental Strengths and Losses at Gettysburg.* Hightstown, NJ: Longstreet House, 1994.

Conklin, George W. "The Long March to Steven's Run: The 134th New York Volunteer Infantry at Gettysburg." *The Gettysburg Magazine,* No 21 [July 1999), pp. 45–56.

Conklin, George W. *Under the Crescent and Star: The 134th New York Volunteer Infantry in the Civil War.* Port Reading, NJ: Axworthy Publishing, 1999.

Hagan, Edward A. *Hot Whiskey for Five: Schoharie County and the Civil War.* Cobleskill, NY: Times-Journal Press, 1985.

Levey, William T. *The Blue and the Gray: A Sketch of Soldier Life in Camp and Field in the Army of the Potomac in the Army of the Civil War.* Schenectady, NY: Roy Burton Myers, 1904.

Photographs

C.C. Howard

Major General Oliver Otis Howard commanded the 11th Corps at both Chancellorsville and Gettysburg. A strict disciplinarian, Howard's stern and uncompromising leadership was not enough to impose order on his unfortunate army corps. The unit had the misfortune of being placed in untenable positions at Chancellorsville and Gettysburg, inspiring a virtual rout of the Union forces.

(Photo: Courtesy of author's collection)

Private Amenzo Cady served in
Company C of the 134th New York
Infantry. He was wounded at Resaca,
Georgia, on May 15, 1864, and again
at Peach Tree Creek, Georgia, on July
20, 1864. He was discharged with the
Regiment in 1865.

*(Photo: Courtesy of New York State Military
Museum and Veterans Research Center)*

Lieutenant Charles T. Hunter served in Companies I and E of the 134th New York Infantry. He drowned following a boat accident in the North River in New York City while on recruiting duty on March 11, 1864.

(Photo: Courtesy of New York State Military Museum and Veterans Research Center)

Corporal (later Sergeant) Lewis
Campbell served in Company H of
the 134th New York Infantry but
transferred to the Veterans Reserve
Corps in September 1863 when his
rheumatism proved too much for him.
Campbell later returned to active duty
with the Regiment and was discharged
in 1865.

*(Photo: Courtesy of New York State Military
Museum and Veterans Research Center)*

Private Edward P. Brown was 18 years old when he enlisted in Company H of the 134th New York Infantry. He was discharged with the Regiment in 1865.

(Photo: Courtesy of New York State Military Museum and Veterans Research Center)

Private Ebenezer Rifenbeck served in Company C of the 134th New York Infantry. He was wounded in the right leg and the lung on July 1, 1863, at Gettysburg. He transferred to the Veterans Reserve Corps in 1864.

(Photo: Courtesy of New York State Military Museum and Veterans Research Center)

Corporal Isaac R. Brown served in Company H of the 134th New York Infantry with William Levey. He enlisted at Esperance, New York, at age 20 and survived the war to be discharged with the regiment in 1865.

(Photo: Courtesy of New York State Military Museum and Veterans Research Center)

Corporal Loran Chilson served with
Private Levey in Company H of the
134th New York Infantry. He was
18 when he enlisted. Wounded by
a shell fragment during the Civil
War, he survived his wounds and was
discharged with the regiment in 1865.

*(Photo: Courtesy of New York State Military
Museum and Veterans Research Center)*

Sergeant Amos Humiston of the 154th New York Infantry
was mortally wounded at Gettysburg on July 1, 1863,
and died holding this photograph of his three children.
The image was reproduced in a Philadelphia newspaper
in October 1863. When Humiston's wife heard about the
photo, she was put in contact with officials who were then
able to identify the soldier's remains.

(Photo: Courtesy of author's collection)